A LITTLE DROP OF COURAGE

Hayley Kaye

Copyright © 2024 by Hayley Haye Mathie
All rights reserved.

Published by Familius LLC, www.familius.com
PO Box 1249, Reedley, CA 93654

Familius books are available at special discounts for bulk purchases,
whether for sales promotions or for family or corporate use.
For more information, contact Familius Sales at orders@familius.com.

Reproduction of this book in any manner, in whole or in part,
without written permission of the publisher is prohibited.

Library of Congress Control Number: 2023948840

Print ISBN 9781641709736
EPUB ISBN 9781641708500
Kindle ISBN 9781641708494
Fixed PDF ISBN 9781641708487

Printed in China

Edited by Abigail W. Tree
Cover design by Hayley Mathie
Book layout by Carlos Mireles-Guerrero

10 9 8 7 6 5 4 3 2 1

First Edition

THROUGH THIS BOOK MAY YOU...

Compassionately discover your own definition of courage

so that you may live courageously in whatever way feels authentic to you—

each and every day.

YOU'RE HUMAN

It's normal to...

Be sad from time to time for no reason	Not have everything together	Feel unsure, confused, or not know

Feel ugly some days and cute other days	Be unprepared for how things turned out	Have tough days

Not always be happy	Be more productive on some days and less on others	Fluctuate in weight

YOU CAN	AND STILL
be SCARED	be STRONG
CARE	have BOUNDARIES
be EXCITED	be SAD
REST	be HARD-WORKING
be HOPEFUL	QUESTION

BUT WHAT IF IT WORKS OUT?

IT'S NOT TOO LATE TO...

Learn something new

Try again

Apologize

Decide what YOU want for your life

Reach out to an old friend

Choose a different path

Change your habits or your mindset

| To change your mind | To take a break | To be scared of the unknown |

| To ask for help | **AN ENORMOUS LIST OF** |

| To disappoint people | To love, dislike, or appreciate your body | To have a bad day |

THINGS THAT ARE TOTALLY OKAY

- To fail
- To not want the same things as other people, even your family
- To make a mistake
- To disagree
- To be sad, happy, unsure, and sometimes all at the same time
- To not know all the answers... or any answers
- To not fit in

SOMETIMES HEALING

Saying "no" without guilt when you don't really want to do something

Feeling calm in places and moments where you used to feel triggered

Getting curious about your feelings rather than trying to numb, push down, or create a story

LOOKS LIKE...

Pausing before responding instead of instantly reacting

Crying without shame

Holding space for others' feelings without rushing to diminish, solve, or advise

Getting triggered and remembering that healing isn't linear and this moment doesn't void all the progress you've made

STOP GASLIGHTING YOURSELF

 Maybe it's all in my head

 My experiences are real and valid

 I shouldn't feel this way

 If it's sticking with me, it must be a trigger. Where do I need to heal?

 I shouldn't be upset. I'm sure they didn't mean it

 Even if they didn't mean to be unkind, it still hurt

 I don't deserve to be happy

 My past mistakes don't define my future

YOU ARE STRONGER THAN WHAT YOU'RE FACING

YOU STILL MATTER

even if you're not...

On a "30 Under 30" list

A certain size, shape, or height

ve a 5/10/20-year plan

Perfect

Always invited

Outgoing

Even 5% sure what you're doing

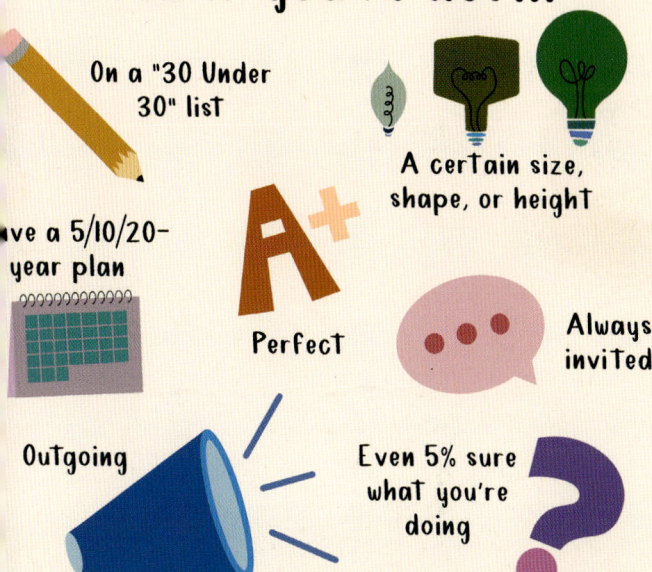

BEING HUMAN 101

Sometimes you'll feel sad for no reason

The feelings you resist are the feelings that will persist

No one has it all figured out

What makes you weird is your superpower. Own it

How you speak to yourself will determine your day, week, and year

Even with the best intentions, you can make mistakes

Hard days don't determine your life

Even when it feels li it, you're not alone

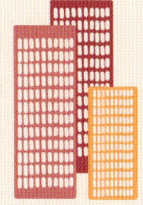

Laugh in the places you cried

Take selfies in the places you felt ugly

Sing where you felt voiceless

TAKE BACK THE NARRATIVE

Dream where they made you doubt

Expand where they told you to shrink

Dance in the places you were breaking

WHEN YOU FEEL STUCK...

- Try a new route to work
- Watch a show you would normally never pick out
- Rearrange a room
- Take a class you've never considered
- Go to a local event and push yourself to meet 3 new people
- Volunteer somewhere new
- Try foods that you think you hate but haven't had in a long time

30 Days of

SELF-COMPASSION

16 Get curious about the root of your self-doubt	17 Tell someone you appreciate them	18 Cry	19 Push yourself a little outside your comfort zone
20 Take responsibility for any mistakes you've made	21 Say "no" and mean it	22 Sit in silence for 5 minutes	23 Accept a compliment without questioning
24 Question if fear is leading your life or your goals	25 Sincerely apologize to someone you have hurt	26 Let go of control and let life flow	27 Do something younger you would be excited about
	28 Write down 5 reminders for when times get tough	29 Do one thing your doubt tells you you can't do	30 Rest without determining if you deserve it (you do!)

Self-Care Doesn't Have to Be Solo

- Read books together in the park
- Take a nature walk together after work
- Watch your favorite TV show together over video chat
- Do something your inner children would be ecstatic about
- Listen and let one another feel all their emotions without judgment
- Have regular, honest check-ins with one another

5-MINUTE SELF-REFLECTION

 Am I responding right now from a place of love or hurt?

 Are the choices for my life a reflection of my values or others' values?

 Would I feel comfortable with others talking to me the way I'm talking to myself right now?

 Am I meeting people where they are at in their own unique story, or am I judging their choices based on my own beliefs and experiences?

 Am I living in this moment from a place of truth or a story I've made up in my head?

THERE'S NOTHING WRONG WITH YOU FOR NOT HAVING IT ALL FIGURED OUT

THINGS THAT CHANGED MY MENTAL HEALTH

Letting myself feel my feelings without judgment

Giving myself permission to take breaks without feeling pressure to always hustle

Moving my body daily in whatever way that works for me for however long feels good

Making manageable lists to organize my day

Giving myself space to be silly without inhibition

Giving myself grace when my to-do list isn't perfectly completed

RANDOM ACTS OF KINDNESS

Send a loved one money for takeout or cook for them

Pick up trash during your daily walk

Offer help to someone who may be lost or confused

Give a genuine compliment to a stranger

If you see someone crying, offer to get them water or to be a listening ear

Apologize to someone you've hurt, even if its been awhile

Ask a friend who has been struggling to join you for a fun night

Asking for help

Speaking compassionately to yourself

Saying "no" in order to honor your well-being

SOMETIMES "HANDLING IT" LOOKS LIKE...

Letting yourself cry without judgment

Owning your mistakes and apologizing where needed

Resting

TALK A LITTLE NICER TO YOURSELF TODAY

SMALL PROMISES I MAKE EVERY MORNING

I promise to show up for myself without needing to convince others that I deserve to

I promise not to compare my life to others' lives and trust that I'm on the right track

I promise to give myself a breather when things become stressful

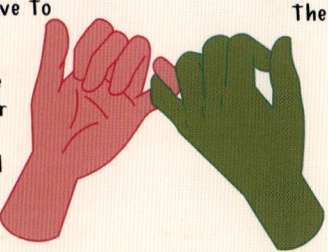

I promise to always choose kindness, even when life isn't kind

I promise to still believe in myself, even when I'm not perfect

I promise to lean in to whatever my best looks like for me today and trust that it is enough

PICK-ME-UP
Reminders

Your voice matters.
Your perspective matters.
You matter.

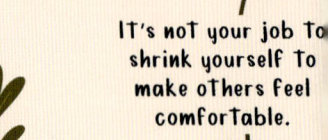

It's not your job to shrink yourself to make others feel comfortable.

How you feel now is not how you'll always feel. Let life ebb and flow.

Self-confidence comes from celebrating ALL your wins, even the small ones that are not recognized by others.

Stop questioning if you're good enough and start stating that you ARE good enough. The first will hold you back; the second will push you to try.

IT'S OKAY TO...

Say "no" in order to take care of yourself

Need help

Be a work in progress

Ask for help

Have a range of feelings and emotions

Not have it all together

Mess up or fail

Cry

Change your mind

SPEAK LIKE YOU ARE

You know how much you've gone through to get here. You're allowed to celebrate this win, regardless if anyone else understands.

It's okay to be scared. You've still absolutely got this!

I know it's been really, really hard. It's okay to cry and ask for help. That doesn't undermine how strong you are.

YOUR BEST FRIEND

You've been showing up for everyone. It's okay to start showing up for yourself.

Sure, maybe it won't work out. OR maybe it will work out better than you ever imagined! Only one way to find out.

Who cares what they think? Do YOU like you? Are YOU proud of yourself? Are YOU happy with your life? That's all that matters.

Let the record show that I was not perfect, but I tried my very best every day.

MAKE SURE YOUR TO-DO LISTS INCLUDE TIMES TO REST AND RECOVER

30 Days of

1 Give yourself permission to feel your feels

2 Notice what triggers you

3 Become aware of your patterns

4 Speak kindly to yourself about your past

9 Get curious where any self-doubt comes in

10 Do something that brings you joy

11 Grieve an apology you never received

12 Clean a small space in your home

17 Focus your energy on what can go right

18 Apologize to someone you've hurt

19 Open yourself up to change

20 Donate what doesn't bring you joy

25 Do something fun with a friend

26 Laugh, even for no reason

27 Say "no" without worry

HEALING

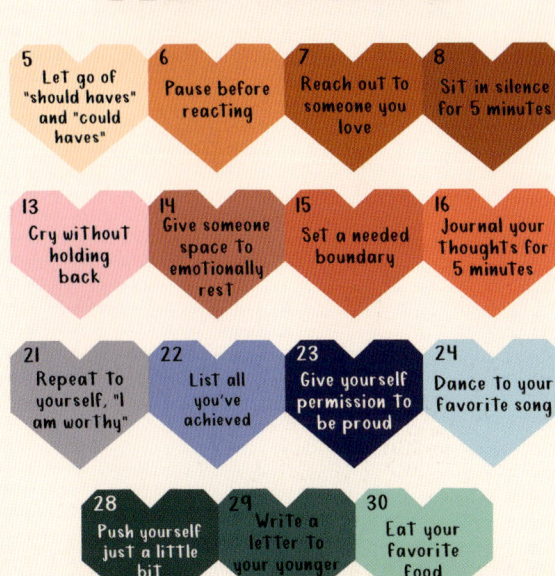

- 5. Let go of "should haves" and "could haves"
- 6. Pause before reacting
- 7. Reach out to someone you love
- 8. Sit in silence for 5 minutes
- 13. Cry without holding back
- 14. Give someone space to emotionally rest
- 15. Set a needed boundary
- 16. Journal your thoughts for 5 minutes
- 21. Repeat to yourself, "I am worthy"
- 22. List all you've achieved
- 23. Give yourself permission to be proud
- 24. Dance to your favorite song
- 28. Push yourself just a little bit
- 29. Write a letter to your younger self
- 30. Eat your favorite food

MONDAY REMINDERS

Your value doesn't decrease based on someone's inability to see your worth.

You are already enough just as you are.

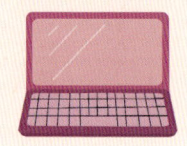

Not all thoughts deserve attention.

How others treat you is a reflection of them, not you.

Your worth doesn't depend on how busy you are.

It's totally OKAY if you...

- Have a bad day
- Change your mind
- Feel lost
- Are sad
- Dislike your body
- Have a mental illness

Life is not constant
IT EBBS AND FLOWS...

Some seasons are joyful; some seasons are painful

Friendships come and go

Some days things come easy to you, and other days nothing does

Your body can be out of trend and then in

Careers can be fulfilling for a season and not in another

What excites you today might not excite you tomorrow

STOP OVER-THINKING IT

It will be okay.

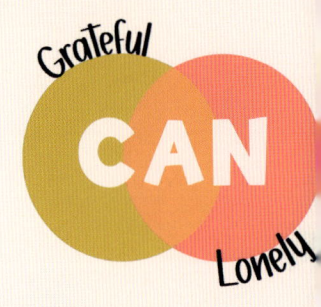

YOU — Anxious, Hopeful

CAN — Grateful, Lonely

BE — Excited, Sad

BOTH — Happy, Angry

GIVE YOURSELF SPACE TO FEEL!

It doesn't have to be long
Even 2 minutes can help!

Vent it out
Talk, Write, Paint, Walk

No judgment
You don't have to figure out why or how right now. Just feel

Be honest with yourself and say it like it is
"This sucks!"
"I'm scared."
"UGH!!"

STOP SHOULDING YOURSELF

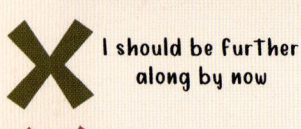

✗ I should be further along by now	✓ I'm right on track for my own path
✗ I should do what makes them happy	✓ I don't have to live up othersʼ expectations
✗ I should look more like them	✓ I don't need to look li[ke] anyone else but myse[lf]
✗ I should be working harder, longer	✓ I am allowed to listen t[o] my body and take breaks when I need to
✗ I shouldn't be thinking about what I need	✓ It is not selfish to ta[ke] care of myself

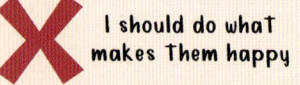

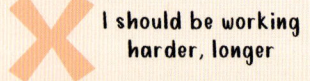

You are enough

You have always been enough

You will always be a ridiculous amount of enough

SOMETIMES SELF-CARE LOOKS LIKE...

- Sitting in your parked car for a little longer
- Putting your favorite song on repeat
- Taking a few extra minutes in the shower
- Taking a long walk
- Making cookies without guilt
- Rereading old texts that made you smile

THE YEARS MAY CHANGE BUT YOUR WORTH DOESN'T

STICKY NOTE REMINDERS

- Taking a break isn't selfish. It's self-care
- It's okay to have hard days. It doesn't mean you're failing
- You don't have to face your battles alone
- You are worthy, even when you don't feel like it
- Others' opinions of you are not your responsibility
- Don't make life-changing decisions with momentary feelings

YOU DESERVE TO KNOW...

YOU MATTER
as more than a giver to others. You matter for just who you are.

YOU'RE LOVED,
not because of what you do but because you're an incredible human.

YOU'RE WORTHY
of being cared for, not because of what you provide but because you are enough.

EVEN IF...
you don't believe any of this right now, you deserve to know it's still true.

No matter our shape, color, or size,

we're worthy of spectacular lives!

JUST BECAUSE...		DOESN'T MEAN...
You're worried	→	It won't go well
You're unsure if you can	→	You can't
Things have been tough	→	They won't get better
You've been hurt	→	Good Things won't find you
Instrusive Thoughts feel real	→	They are True

YOU DON'T NEED TO BE EXCEPTIONAL TO HAVE AN EXCEPTIONAL LIFE

YOU DON'T NEED TO HAVE IT TOGETHER ALL THE TIME

30 Days of

1 Be patient with yourself when you mess up	**2** Feel without judgment	**3** Look for patterns in your behavior	**4** Search for the root of those patterns
5 Mourn the cause of those patterns	**6** Do something outside your comfort zone	**7** Look for the good in people	**8** Forgive yourself
9 Decide what you think FIRST	**10** Question why you judge others	**11** Do something you've been told you can't	**12** Write down what you like about yourself
13 Write down what you dislike about yourself	**14** Question where that dislike came from	**15** Find the real need beneath the dislike	

SELF-ACCEPTANCE

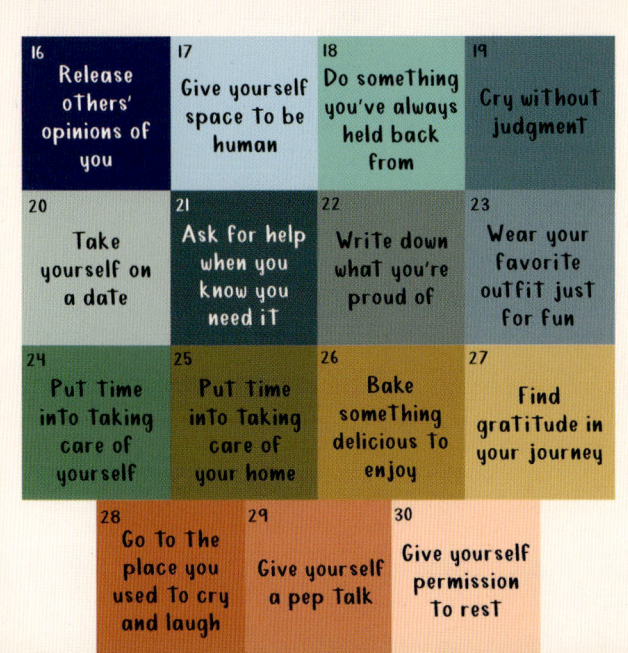

16. Release others' opinions of you	17. Give yourself space to be human	18. Do something you've always held back from	19. Cry without judgment
20. Take yourself on a date	21. Ask for help when you know you need it	22. Write down what you're proud of	23. Wear your favorite outfit just for fun
24. Put time into taking care of yourself	25. Put time into taking care of your home	26. Bake something delicious to enjoy	27. Find gratitude in your journey
28. Go to the place you used to cry and laugh	29. Give yourself a pep talk	30. Give yourself permission to rest	

- Social comparisons
- Those adamant on judging you
- Unsolicited advice
- Social norms that don't align with who you are
- Intrusive Thoughts
- The "should haves," "could haves," and "would haves"

Protect your energy from...

No matter how much you got done this week, you are still...

STRONG

LOVED

CAPABLE

VALUABLE

WORTHY OF KINDNESS

Be honest and say "no" when you don't want to do something

Stand up for yourself

Decide what you think before asking for others' opinions

Even if no one else is cheering, cheer for yourself

SHOW UP FOR YOURSELF

Forgive yourself when you've made a mistake

Prioritize time to do things that bring you joy and peace

Friendly Reminders
EVERYONE HAS...

- Been rejected
- Made a mistake
- Felt alone
- Been hurt
- Said something they regret
- Disappointed someone
- Cried
- Felt left out

You are so much more than the way you look

Telling someone to stop being anxious never makes them feel better.

Asking someone how you can help them could change their life.

STOP BLAMING YOURSELF FOR...

- Not knowing then what you know now
- Not being accepted for being yourself
- Not being perfect
- The choices you made when you were still healing
- Listening to your intrusive thoughts
- The way they treated you

THINGS THAT BRING ME JOY
(When I don't feel very joyful)

- Cozying up in big blankets
- Rereading old texts
- Playing with my cat
- Going on long walks
- Reading a good book
- Looking up at the night sky
- Having a fridge full of food

Turn your mind into your home.
Plant some flowers.
Decorate.
Make it a place
you're at peace
instead of another
battlefield.

SELF-COMPASSION SAYS

- I forgive myself for what I did when I was still learning
- They have a right to turn me down and do what's best for them. It is not a reflection of my worth
- I made a mistake, but I am not a mistake
- Things didn't go as planned, but I can celebrate trying my best from day to day
- I have stuff to work on, but I am worth the work
- I may not be where I want yet, but that doesn't mean I won't get there
- I am not meant to be perfect. I'm human

MENTAL HEALTH KIT

- Water
- Music that sparks joy
- Therapy
- Self-compassion
- Someone you can talk honestly to
- Space to cry without shame
- Something delicious
- Something that gets your body up and moving
- Medication (if necessary)
- Journal

Signs you may be burned out and need a break

- Everything seems to be a bigger deal
- You're struggling to focus
- You're constantly doubting yourself
- Nothing excites you anymore
- Decisions, even the small ones, are hard
- You're exhausted without much physical exertion

EVERY FEELING IS VALID

Instead of
JUST THINK POSITIVE...

- Feel all your feelings so you can move through them
- Embrace the full range of the human experience
- Give yourself permission to fully exist in every mood and season
- Get curious as to what parts of you still need healing
- Be mindful of the stories you're telling yourself
- Release judgment and speak compassionately to yourself

SELF-JUDGMENT

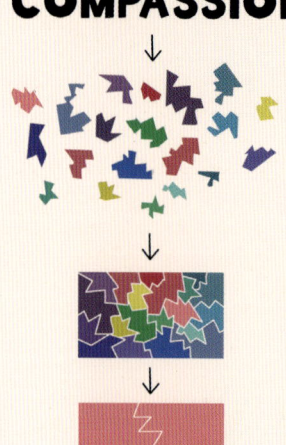

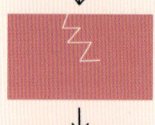

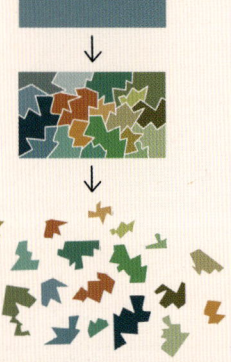

SELF-COMPASSION

THINGS YOU DESERVE TO CELEBRATE

- Overcoming intrusive thoughts
- Putting in time, even 5 minutes, for your mental health
- Encouraging youself
- Giving yourself grace and compassion
- Getting through the week
- Doing the hard things you thought you couldn't do

One of the bravest things you can do is be who you are in a sea of people telling you who you ought to be. Do it boldly and do it anyway.

Heal, even if you never get a chance to apologize.

Heal, even if you never receive an apology.

30 Days of

1 Take a 2-minute break to just breathe	**2** Do something new just for fun	**3** Release the pressure and give yourself grace	**4** Do a random act of kindness
5 Go for a walk	**6** Do a chore you've been putting off	**7** Let yourself feel without judgment	**8** Speak kindly to yourself
9 Clean a small space in your home	**10** Donate anything you no longer want or use	**11** Say "no" to something you really don't want to do	**12** Write 2 affirmations to repeat to yourself daily
13 Do something you've been too scared to do	**14** Celebrate how far you've come for 3 minutes	**15** Try a new recipe	

SELF-CARE

16 Set one boundary where you're feeling drained	**17** Grieve the apology you never received	**18** Apologize where you may need to	**19** Check in on a friend
20 Have a solo dance party to your favorite song	**21** Write out all your thoughts without judgment	**22** Go to bed an hour early	**23** Put encouraging reminders on your mirrors
24 Say 3 things you LOVE about your body	**25** Have an open and honest conversation with someone	**26** Do something younger you would be excited about	**27** Take a fun online class
	28 Support a cause you believe in	**29** Ask for help where you know you need it	**30** Show up and stand up for yourself

Give compassion where you received hate

YOU'VE GOT THIS!

Offer encouragement where you've been shamed

BREAK THE CYCLE

Spread joy where you've been rejected

Have patience where you've been pressured

Be a listening ear where you've been silenced

Embrace your worth where you've been denied

WHOEVER MADE YOU DOUBT YOURSELF IS WRONG. THEY ARE DOUBTING YOU FROM THE LENS OF THEIR OWN INSECURITY. AND FRANKLY, THAT'S NONE OF YOUR BUSINESS.

IT'S OKAY TO FEEL

- Angry for what's happening in the world today
- Proud of yourself and your accomplishments
- Devastated for what people are going through
- Ashamed for not knowing more or not knowing the right thing to say
- Unsure if you're doing enough or if it will even make a difference
- Anxious for what will happen to others and and yourself
- Grateful for what you have
- Hopeful that we will come together and help one another

ALL AT ONCE

Break up with Others' expectations

Break up with The idea of how it's supposed to go

Break up with

The belief that you can't

Break up with   Normal

PUSHING DOWN FEELINGS IS EASY UNTIL ONE DAY YOU FIND YOURSELF CRYING TO A SONG THAT REMINDS YOU OF SOMETHING THAT HAPPENED 10 YEARS AGO WITH A PERSON WHOSE NAME YOU DON'T EVEN REMEMBER

Rest means sleep, but it can also mean...

- Going on a long walk
- Ordering take-out
- Listening to music
- Wearing pajamas all day
- Disconnecting from social media
- Binging a TV show

NO MATTER HOW HARD IT GETS, I HOPE YOU STAY OPEN TO...

Opportunties To heal

A genuine helping hand

The idea that being lost means you have something To find

New friends

Your ability to overcome and evolve

Self-compassion and gentleness

The rainbow coming on The other side

HEALING CAN BE HARD, BUT IT CAN ALSO...

- Bring clarity to how the hurt is continuing to affect your day-to-day
- Give you compassion for others and what they're going through
- Put distance between you and the hurt
- Help you see things from other perspectives and not just as you remember them
- Give you space to share your story and provide relief and hope to others
- Give you the freedom to no longer see the hurt as a reflection of you but rather as something that happened to you

ONE OF THE BRAVEST THINGS YOU CAN DO IS BE YOURSELF IN A WORLD THAT'S CONSTANTLY SAYING EVERYTHING ABOUT YOU IS WRONG

You know you've started healing when...

- Comparison feels like a waste of time because everyone is on their own journey
- You stop trying to control how others see you and focus on how you see yourself
- Putting yourself and your mental health first doesn't feel selfish but necessary
- You can look back and be proud of how far you've come
- You're quick to pause and slow to react

HAVE THE COURAGE TO SAY...

- My feelings are not up for discussion
- I don't need to prove myself to you
- I need to do what's best for me
- No (without further explanation)
- I'm not comfortable with this

TO MY YOUNGER SELF,

You are enough just as you are.

Life is hard and messy, and no one has it figured out. But you will find joy that will make it worth living.

You're not crazy or weird or a lot for having big feelings. You're human.

Everyone feels scared, awkward, and self-conscious sometimes.

Don't listen to them. It's not really about you.

You're going to be okay.

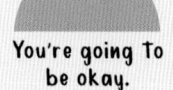

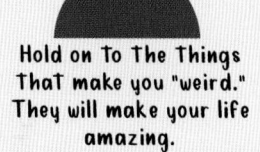

Hold on to the things that make you "weird." They will make your life amazing.

It's called anxiety, and no, it's not just in your head.

You're the only person who will be with you your whole life. Make sure you like them.

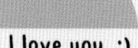

I love you. :)

Boundaries aren't about keeping people out

but what you accept when they come in

PROGRESS LOOKS LIKE...

Don't give up here!
This is still progress!

30 Days of

1. I can handle anything that comes my way
2. I am resilient
3. I keep my mind open to all paths
4. I deserve to care for every part of me
5. It's okay to feel all my feelings
6. Help is always near when I ask for it
7. My past does not predict my future
8. I alone am in control of my body
9. When I seek peace, I find it
10. I am worthy of good things
11. Compassion and kindness flow through me
12. I release the need for perfection
13. I am always enough
14. I choose to keep learning and growing
15. I am worthy of respect

AFFIRMATIONS

- **16.** I am capable of more than I imagined
- **17.** I let go of comparisons
- **18.** I give myself permission to rest
- **19.** I trust myself and my decisions
- **20.** I am brave
- **21.** I can handle anything that comes my way
- **22.** I am worthy of healing
- **23.** I choose to honor my needs
- **24.** I find good all around me
- **25.** I believe in myself
- **26.** I am in control of my life
- **27.** I am strong enough even when I'm scared
- **28.** I release what is not within my control
- **29.** I choose who I become
- **30.** I've got this!

Some years will break you,

Some years will rebuild you,

And some will show you why.

I WILL

NOT COMPARE

MY JOURNEY

Hard-Day Reminders

- 24 hours. A day is only 24 hours
- The day doesn't define you and what you're capable of
- It will get better, even if it doesn't feel like it right now
- It's okay to say this sucks. That doesn't invalidate your ability to overcome
- You've gotten through hard days before. You'll get through this one too

REPEAT DURING A PANIC ATTACK

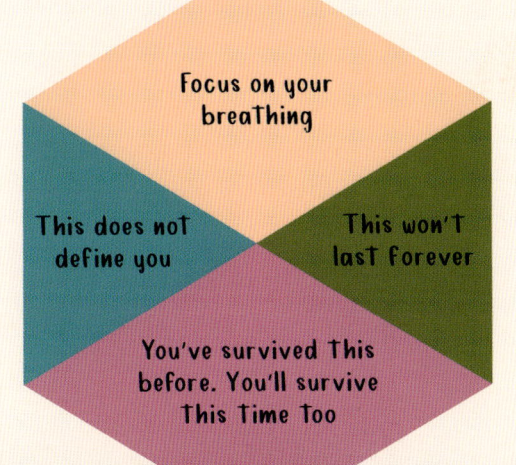

- Focus on your breathing
- This won't last forever
- You've survived this before. You'll survive this time too
- This does not define you

Mental Health Is NOT a Competition

- If you think you've got it bad, I experienced...
- Your day was nothing compared to mine.
- You've got it easy compared to me.
- Stop complaining. I've got it worse, and you don't hear me saying anything.

YOUR INTRUSIVE THOUGHTS ARE LYING TO YOU!

(You're doing just fine!)

THINGS THAT DON'T DETERMINE YOUR VALUE

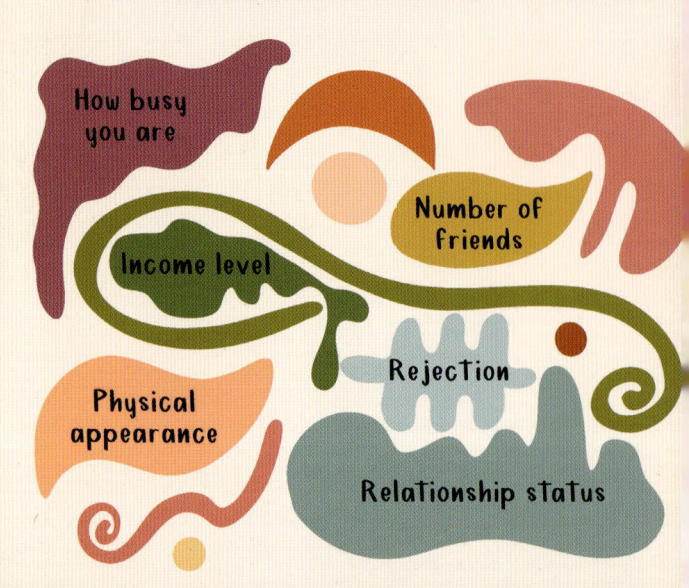

- How busy you are
- Number of friends
- Income level
- Physical appearance
- Rejection
- Relationship status

CELEBRATE THE LOVE BETWEEN...

You + Your favorite food	You + Your best friend
You + Your pet	You + Someone no longer here
You + Your community	You + Yourself

Things you don't have to feel bad about

- Taking a break
- Saying "no"
- Not living up to someone's expectations
- Setting boundarie[s]
- Crying
- Making your mental health a priority

Your healing does not depend on

- Their healing
- Their approval
- Their support
- Their awareness
- Their acknowledgment
- Their acceptance
- Their apology
- Their growth

YOU ARE NOT DEFINED BY YOUR HARD DAYS

Good hasn't finished working its MAGIC on you yet

Friendly Reminders
YOU DON'T HAVE TO...

- Be happy all the time to be liked
- Know yourself to know what is best for you
- Be healed to be loved
- Wait until you're breaking down to ask for help
- Have a title, career, or status to deserve respect
- Love your body to be worthy of being cared for

Instead of
NEW YEAR, NEW ME...

Celebrate all the things you overcame and all the little wins.

Give yourself space to feel all the feels from last year so you can heal (it's okay if this takes time!).

Write down reminders to keep close and read when things get tough.

Reach out to those who've helped you through the year and tell them the impact they've had.

Remind yourself that you don't have to change who you are to have an amazing year. You are already enough.

Listen to your feelings. They are guiding you.

- **Anxiety**: I am doing something brave
- **Loneliness**: I value connection
- **Sadness**: I lost something I cared about
- **Jealousy**: I want more for my life
- **Anger**: I need a boundary here

SOMETIMES THE BEST MEDICINE IS A BIG OL' CRY, AND THAT'S OKAY!

You can't change what happened
BUT YOU CAN...

Forgive yourself for not knowing Then what you know now

Give yourself space to feel so you can heal

Learn from what happened so it doesn't affect how you treat others

Grieve the experience you had wanted

Advocate for change and share your experience to help others

Things worth celebrating this week

- Sticking to your boundaries
- Not letting fear control you
- Pushing yourself just a little bit
- Letting yourself feel
- Pausing instead of reacting
- Giving yourself space to rest when you need it
- Talking compassionately to yourself when you mess up

30 Days of

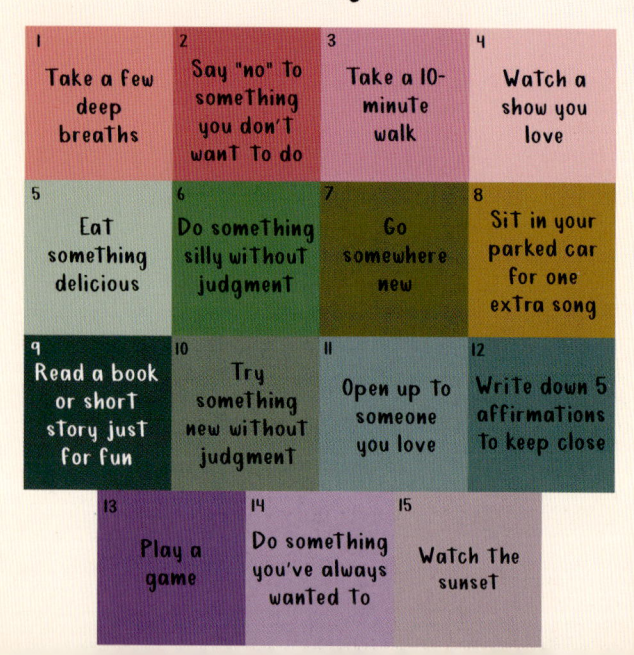

1 Take a few deep breaths	**2** Say "no" to something you don't want to do	**3** Take a 10-minute walk	**4** Watch a show you love
5 Eat something delicious	**6** Do something silly without judgment	**7** Go somewhere new	**8** Sit in your parked car for one extra song
9 Read a book or short story just for fun	**10** Try something new without judgment	**11** Open up to someone you love	**12** Write down 5 affirmations to keep close
	13 Play a game	**14** Do something you've always wanted to	**15** Watch the sunset

REST

16 Volunteer for a cause you believe in	17 Plan a night with friends	18 Have a night with friends	19 Take a class on something you've always wanted to try
20 Find places you need to set strong boundaries	21 Set those boundaries	22 Spend all day in your PJs	23 Journal your thoughts
24 Schedule the doctor's appointment you've been putting off	25 Give yourself space to feel all your feelings	26 Let yourself laugh	27 Listen to your favorite song on repeat
28 Read old texts that make you smile	29 Go on an adventure	30 Take a nice long nap	

ABOUT THE AUTHOR

Hayley Kaye is an illustrator and content creator best known for her colorful and compassionate reminders on Instagram at @iamhayleykaye.

After being diagnosed with anxiety and OCD in her early twenties, she has made it her mission to live more courageously and help others do the same.

ACKNOWLEDGMENTS

To John, my love and best friend, for being my source of strength and encouragement and holding my hand through it all.

To Mom and Dad, for always believing me and picking up my late-night calls.

To Leah, Rita, and Amanda, for your unwavering friendship through the laughs and tears.

To Delphi, my furry companion, who never left my lap throughout the entire creation process.

ABOUT FAMILIUS

Visit Our Website: www.familius.com

Familius is a global trade publishing company that publishes books and other content to help families be happy. We believe that happy families are key to a better society and the foundation of a happy life. The greatest work anyone will ever do will be within the walls of his or her own home. And we don't mean vacuuming! We recognize that every family looks different and passionately believe in helping all families find greater joy, whatever their situation. To that end, we publish beautiful books that help families live our 10 Habits of Happy Family Life: *love together, play together, learn together, work together, talk together, heal together, read together, eat together, give together*, and *laugh together*. Further, Familius does not discriminate on the basis of race, color, religion, gender, age, nationality, disability, caste, or sexual orientation in any of its activities or operations. Founded in 2012, Familius is located in Sanger, California.

Connect

Facebook: www.facebook.com/familiusbooks
Pinterest: www.pinterest.com/familiusbooks
Instagram: @FamiliusBooks
TikTok: @FamiliusBooks